Gangsters, Ghosts and Dragonflies

Brian Patten has published six volumes of poetry (*Little Johnny's Confession, Notes to the Hurrying Man, The Irrelevant Song, Vanishing Trick, Grave Gossip and Love Poems*) and several children's books (including *Emma's Doll, The Elephant and the Flower, Jumping Mouse,* and the award-winning detective story *Mr Moon's Last Case*). His work has been translated into Dutch, German, Italian, Japanese, Polish and Spanish. Besides writing children's books and poetry, he also writes for the theatre and for television.

D0988224

Gangsters, Ghosts and Dragonflies

a book of story poems chosen by
Brian Patten

illustrated by Terry Oakes

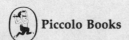 Piccolo Books

First published 1981 by George Allen & Unwin Ltd
This Piccolo edition published 1983 by Pan Books Ltd,
Cavaye Place, London SW10 9PG
© Brian Patten 1981
illustrations © Terry Oakes 1981
ISBN 0 330 26955 0
Printed and bound in Great Britain by
Collins, Glasgow.

Contents

Introduction

No one in their right mind would go out to buy a bottle of sour milk or a loaf of stale bread, and I wouldn't expect anyone to buy a book of sour poems or an anthology of stale verse. In *Gangsters, Ghosts and Dragonflies* it has been my aim to gather together the work of contemporary poets whose poems are inventive and fresh, and so create a book which bridges the gap between collections for younger readers and those for adults. With a few notable exceptions the poems are all by living poets.

In one way or another the poems in this anthology tell a story, and I have chosen them because poems of this kind are the most accessible of all. Whether allegories, fables or simply fun, I hope they will be remembered and enjoyed.

So come on in and visit the Forest of Tangle; meet the Man-Moth, Oilcan Harry and the apeman who hated snakes. Mrs Blow is here, dancing with her animals, and so is Miss Bigelow (who chewed the postman's ear) and George (who spat at dragonflies); not to mention five hundred naked men, a new cat, a lost knee, a berserk rocking-horse and a wild Yorkshire pudding – and other unexpected things.

Brian Patten

Oilcan Harry

Oilcan Harry, feeling bored,
Tied his sister to a Ford.
Harry chuckled at the gag.
Sister found it quite a drag.

Oilcan Harry used to cram
His brothers underneath the tram.
'Gosh,' he grumbled, 'Heaven sakes,
Why should they get all the breaks?'

Oilcan Harry never meant
To drown his dad to that extent:
He only kept him in the tank
Because the tar and feathers stank.

Oilcan Harry drew the line –
Up and down his uncle's spine.
He used sulphuric, I might say.
Uncle's spineless to this day.

The day she died, just on a hunch,
Harry had his mum for lunch.
Now he can't sit down to sup
Without bringing Mother up.

Oilcan Harry met his doom
Building bombs in the living room:
When he saw he'd made a goof,
Oilcan Harry hit the roof.

Dennis Lee

You'd better believe him

A Fable

He discovered an old rocking-horse in Woolworth's,
He tried to feed it but without much luck.
So he stroked it, had a long conversation about
The trees it came from, the attics it had visited.
Tried to take it out then
But the store detective he
Called the store manager who
Called the police who in court next morning said
'He acted strangely when arrested,
His statement read simply "I believe in rocking-horses."
We have reason to believe him mad.'
'Quite so,' said the prosecution,
'Bring in the rocking-horse as evidence.'
'I'm afraid it's escaped, sir,' said the store manager,
'Left a hoof-print as evidence
On the skull of the store detective.'
'Quite so,' said the prosecution, fearful
of the neighing
Out in the corridor.

Brian Patten

The apeman who hated snakes

Was an apeman lived next door to me
In some kind of prickly tree.

That apeman had the angry shakes
Spending all his sleep in dreams about snakes.

And every morning he would shout
How all the snakes have to be stamp out.

Pastime he enjoy the best
Was to poke a stick down a mamba's nest

Or he'd have a slaughter down the old snake-pit
And look pretty happy at the end of it.

He tattooed snakes all over his skin
Coiling and hissing from knees to chin.

For breakfast he hard-boiled the eggs of snakes.
Suppertime – Boa-constrictor steaks.

For a man who hated reptiles so obsessively
He spend an awful lot of time in their company.

Now where that apeman lived next door to me
There's a vacancy in that prickly tree.

I reckon snakes are like me and you –
They got a mystery job to do.

So when I see one in my path I salute
And take a roundabout alternative route.

Adrian Mitchell

Vague impressions

Ossie Edwards couldn't punch a hole in a wet echo.
He was no fighter.
And if he wasn't thicker than 2 short planks
he wasn't much brighter.
To compensate, he did impressions.
Impressions of trains, impressions of planes,
of James Cagney, Humphrey Bogart and Roy Rogers.
They all sounded the same.
On the 3rd year Cosa Nostra
his impressions made little impression
so he became bully fodder.

Then, quite suddenly, Ossie saw the light.
One Monday morning during R.I.
he switched to birdcalls.
Peewits, kestrels, tomtits and kingfishers
he became them all.
Larks and nightingales.
The birdnotes burst from his throat
like a host of golden buckshot.
And as the nearest any of us got to ornithology
was playing football on a debris with a dead pigeon
there could be no argument.
So he was rechristened 'Percy'
and left alone.
And left alone
he twittered his way happily to 3 'O' levels
and a job in a shipping office.

'Twas there he met Sylvia
whom he courted and married.
She took an interest in his hobby
and they were soon appearing in local concerts:
'The Sylvatones – Bird Impressionists'.
The double-act ended however
when Sylvia left him for a widower
who taught her how to sing.
Her love for Perce she realized
never was the real thing,
but, like his impressions, a tuneful imitation.

And that was years ago and still
whenever I pass that way at night
and hear the shrill
yearning hoot of an owl,
I imagine Percy
perched out there in the darkness,
lonely, obsessed.
Calling for his love
to return to the nest.

Roger McGough

A motorbike

We had a motorbike all through the war
In an outhouse – thunder, flight, disruption
Cramped in rust, under washing, abashed, outclassed
By the Brens, the Bombs, the Bazookas elsewhere.

The war ended, the explosions stopped.
The men surrendered their weapons
And hung around limply.
Peace took them all prisoner.
They were herded into their home towns.
A horrible privation began
Of working a life up out of the avenues
And the holiday resorts and the dance-halls.

Then the morning bus was as bad as any labour truck,
The foreman, the boss, as bad as the SS
And the ends of the street and the bends of the road
And the shallowness of the shops and the shallowness of
    the beer
And the sameness of the next town
Were as bad as electrified barbed wire.
The shrunk-back war ached in their testicles
And England dwindled to the size of a dog-track.

So there came this quiet young man
And he bought our motorbike for twelve pounds.
And he got it going, with difficulty.
He kicked into life – it erupted
Out of the six-year sleep, and he was delighted.

A week later, astride it, before dawn,
A misty frosty morning,
He escaped

Into a telegraph pole
On the long straight west of Swinton.

Ted Hughes

The National Health Cow

I strolled into a farmyard
When no one was about
Treading past the troubles
I raised my head to shout.

'Come out the Cow with glasses,'
I called and rolled my eye.
It ambled up towards me,
I milked it with a sigh.

'You're just in time,' the cow said,
Its eyes were all aglaze,
'I'm feeling like an elephant,
I aren't been milked for days.'

'Why is this?' I asked it,
Tugging at its throttles.
'I don't know why, perhaps it's 'cause
MY milk comes out in bottles.'

'That's handy for the government,'
I thought, and in a tick
The cow fell dead all sudden
(*I'd smashed it with a brick*).

John Lennon

Growing pain

The boy was barely five years old.
We sent him to the little school
And left him there to learn the names
Of flowers in jam jars on the sill
And learn to do as he was told.
He seemed quite happy there until
Three weeks afterwards, at night,
The darkness whimpered in his room.
I went upstairs, switched on his light,
And found him wide awake, distraught,
Sheets mangled and his eiderdown
Untidy carpet on the floor.
I said, 'Why can't you sleep? A pain?'
He snuffled, gave a little moan,
And then he spoke a single word:
'Jessica.' The sound was blurred.
'Jessica? What do you mean?'
'A girl at school called Jessica,
She hurts – ' he touched himself between
The heart and stomach '– she has been
Aching here and I can see her.'
Nothing I had read or heard
Instructed me in what to do.
I covered him and stroked his head.
'The pain will go, in time,' I said.

Vernon Scannell

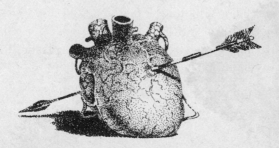

A doll's house

A man sat staring at a doll's house
Hour after hour and more and more
He believed. He could see
In the kitchenette two personettes
And one of them was standing in the sink
And one lay on the floor.

The man stared more and more.

The bed in the bathroom was neatly made up with a
Pink eiderdown neatly made up from a
Pink ribbon. But no one was in the bed
And no one was in the bathroom.
Only a horse
Was trying the door.

The man stared more and more.

Then softly the man went in,
Edged down
Past the creaky banisters, down
He crept
To the hall, hid nimbly
Behind a cow.

From the sink: 'My dear,
That tractor's on the roof again, I fear.'
Sadly from the floor: 'These nights
It seems to be always there.'

Then silence between
Personette A and Personette B,
Now like a matchstick drumming a plastic thimble,
Now like the sea.

From the sink: 'How I wish, my dear,
That you and I could move house.
But these matters are not in our hands. Our directives
Come from above.'
Said the floor: 'How can we ever move house
When the house keeps moving, my love?'

A man sat staring at a doll's house
Hour after hour and more and more
He believed he could see
Perspectives of the terrorized world,
Delicate, as a new-tooled body,
Monstrous, mad as he.

Kit Wright

The meadow mouse

I

In a shoe-box stuffed in an old nylon stocking
Sleeps the baby mouse I found in the meadow,
Where he trembled and shook beneath a stick
Till I caught him up by the tail and brought him in,
Cradled in my hand,
A little quaker, the whole body of him trembling,
His absurd whiskers sticking out like a cartoon-mouse,
His feet like small leaves,
Little lizard-feet,
Whitish and spread wide when he tried to struggle away,
Wriggling like a minuscule puppy.

Now he's eaten his three kinds of cheese and drunk from
  his bottle-cap watering-trough –

So much he just lies in one corner,
His tail curled under him, his belly big
As his head; his bat-like ears
Twitching, tilting towards the least sound.

Do I imagine he no longer trembles
When I come close to him?
He seems no longer to tremble.

II

But this morning the shoe-box house on the back porch is
  empty.
Where has he gone, my meadow mouse,
My thumb of a child that nuzzled in my palm? –
To run under the hawk's wing,
Under the eye of the great owl watching from the elm-tree,
To live by courtesy of the shrike, the snake, the tom-cat.

I think of the nestling fallen into the deep grass,
The turtle gasping in the dusty rubble of the highway,
The paralytic stunned in the tub, and the water rising –
All things innocent, hapless, forsaken.

Theodore Roethke

On Tuesdays I polish my uncle

I went to play in the park.
I didn't get home until dark.
But when I got back I had ants in my pants
And my father was feeding the shark.

I went to play in the park,
And I didn't come home until dark.
And when I got back I had ants in my pants
And dirt in my shirt, and glue in my shoe,
And my father was tickling the shark.

I went to sleep in the park.
The shark was starting to bark.
And when I woke up I had ants in my pants,
Dirt in my shirt, glue in my shoe,
And beans in my jeans and a bee on my knee,
And the shark was tickling my father.

My father went off to the park.
I stayed home and read to the shark.
And when he got back he had ants in his pants,
Dirt in his shirt, glue in his shoe,
Beans in his jeans, a bee on his knee,
Beer in his ear and a bear in his hair,
So we put him outside in the ark.

I started the ark in the dark.
My father was parking the shark.
And when we got home we had ants in our pants,
Dirt in our shirt, glue in our shoe,
Beans in our jeans, a bee on our knee,
Beer in our ear and a bear in our hair,
A stinger in our finger, a stain in our brain,
And our belly-buttons shone in the dark.

So my dad he got snarky and barked at the shark
Who was parking the ark on the mark in the dark.
And when they got back they had ants in their pants,
Dirt in their shirt, glue in their shoe,
Beans in their jeans, a bee on their knee,
Beer in their ear and a bear in their hair,
A stinger in each finger, a stain in the brain,
A small polka-dot burp, with headache tablets,
And a ship on the lip and a horse, of course,
So we all took a bath in the same tub and went to bed early.

Dennis Lee

The sparrow and
the kangaroo

Behind the fence, the kangaroo
has on a sparrow cast his view.

The sparrow perches on the pale –
he doesn't feel too hap and hale.

Uneasily he feels, instead,
the mammal's gaze and ducks his head.

The sparrow ruffles up his wings –
he doesn't trust the look of things.

A terror threatens to unseat him:
What if the kangaroo should eat him?

The latter, though, will briefly pause,
then turn his head, perhaps for cause

(or possibly without reflection)
unto a different direction.

Christian Morgenstern

What the littlegirl did

The littlegirl
   pulled up her bellyskin
      like a vest
         and examined her chest
            spleen, kidneys and the rest
               as a measled child a rash.

Sugar and spice
   and everything nice
      that's what little girls are made of

So she put in a hand
   and pulled out a gland
      and said: 'What a strange girl am I'

Roger McGough

My hat

Mother said if I wore this hat
I should be certain to get off with the right sort of chap
Well look where I am now, on a desert island
With so far as I can see no one at all on hand
I know what has happened though I suppose Mother
    wouldn't see
This hat being so strong has completely run away with me
I had the feeling it was beginning to happen the moment I
    put it on
What a moment that was as I rose up, I rose up like a flying
    swan
As strong as a swan too, why see how far my hat has flown
    me away
It took us a night to come and then a night and a day
And all the time the swan wing in my hat waved beautifully
Ah, I thought, How this hat becomes me.
First the sea was dark but then it was pale blue
And still the wing beat and we flew and we flew
A night and a day and a night, and by the old right way
Between the sun and the moon we flew until morning day.
It is always early morning here on this peculiar island
The green grass grows into the sea on the dipping land
Am I glad I am here? Yes, well, I am,
It's nice to be rid of Father, Mother and the young man
There's just one thing causes me a twinge of pain,
If I take my hat off, shall I find myself home again?
So in this early morning land I always wear my hat
Go home, you see, well I wouldn't run a risk like that.

Stevie Smith

Nothingmas Day

No it wasn't.

It was Nothingmas Eve and all the children in Notown were not tingling with excitement as they lay unawake in their heaps

D
  o
    w
      n
        s
         t
           a
            i
              r

s their parents were busily not placing the last crackermugs, glimmerslips and sweetlumps on the Nothingmas Tree.

HEY! but what was that invisible trail of chummy sparks or vaulting stars across the sky?

Father Nothingmas – drawn by 18 or 21 rainmaidens –
Father Nothingmas – his sackbut bulging with air –
Father Nothingmas – was not on his way.

(From the streets of the snowless town came the quiet of unsung carols and the merry silence of the steeple bell).

Next morning the children did not fountain out of bed with cries of WHOOPERATION! They picked up their Nothingmas stockings and with traditional quiperamas such as: 'Look what I haven't got! It's just what I didn't want!' pulled their stockings on their ordinary legs.

For breakfast they ate breakfast.

After woods they all avoided the Nothingmas Tree, where
Daddy, his face failing to beam like a leaky torch, was not
distributing gemgames, sodaguns, golly-trolleys, jars of
humdrums and packets of slubberated croakers.

Off, off, off went the children to school, soaking each
other with no howls of 'Merry Nothingmas and a Happy No
Year' and not pulping each other with no-balls.

At school Miss Whatnot taught them how to write No
Thank You letters.

Home they burrowed for Nothingmas dinner.

> The table was not groaning under all manner of
> NO TURKEY
> NO SPICED HAM
> NO SPROUTS
> NO CRANBERRY JELLYSAUCE
> NO NOT NOWT.
> There was not one (1) shoot of glee as the
> Nothingmas Pudd
> unlit, was not brought in. Mince pies were not
> available, nor was any demand for them.
>
> Then, as another Nothingmas clobbered to a close,
> they all haggled off to bed where they slept happily
> never after.

Adrian Mitchell

Hector the collector

Hector the collector
Collected bits of string,
Collected dolls with broken heads
And rusty bells that would not ring.
Pieces out of picture puzzles,
Bent-up nails and ice cream sticks,
Twists of wires, worn out tyres,
Paper bags and broken bricks.
Old chipped vases, half shoelaces,
Gatlin' guns that wouldn't shoot,
Leaky boats that wouldn't float
And stopped-up horns that wouldn't toot.
Butter knives that had no handles,
Copper keys that fit no locks,
Rings that were too small for fingers,

Dried-up leaves and patched-up socks.
Worn-out belts that had no buckles,
'Lectric trains that had no tracks,
Airplane models, broken bottles,
Three-legged chairs and cups with cracks.
Hector the collector
Loved these things with all his soul –
Loved them more than shining diamonds,
Loved them more than glistenin' gold.
Hector called to all the people,
'Come and share my treasure trunk',
And all the silly sightless people
Came and looked . . . and called it junk.

Shel Silverstein

The worm and the angel

One night I dreamed that I was dead
a butterfly flew into my head.
'How do you do?' she said
'I'm an Angel'

She said no more she said no less
I said 'Can you get me out of this mess?
If you can well then I guess
you must be an Angel'

Just then a worm crawled up my nose
and said to the butterfly 'I suppose
you think because of your beautiful clothes
you're an Angel!'

The butterfly smiled a knowing smile
and said 'A miss is as good as a mile'
Nothing on earth can cramp the style
of an Angel!

But the worm said 'I'm not satisfied
and if you'd kindly step outside
in a civilized way we can soon decide
who's an Angel!'

Well I was turning in my grave
and the worm began to rant and rave
while the butterfly did not behave
like an Angel.

Then I awoke and found them gone.
I looked at the trees and the morning sun
and wondered if the worm had won
or the Angel?

It's not every day you see the light
but after such a restless night
I knew that only a worm could fight
an Angel.

Neil Innes

Mrs Blow and her animals

There was a dog called Clanworthy
Who lived with his friend the cat Hopdance
In the house of Mrs Blow, a widow,
Upon a glade in Cluny.

Hey, Hopdance,
How is Mrs Blow?
So-so, said Hopdance,
Bow, said the dog.

Mrs Blow
Loved her animals very much
She often said:
I do not know what I should do
Without Hopdance and
Clanworthy.

They loved her too.

Hey, Hopdance,
How is Mrs Blow?
So-so, said Hopdance,
She is not very well, said the dog.

Hopdance fetched her a fish
Which she cooked by the fire.
That will do her good,
Said Hopdance; but, said the dog,
She must have wine as well as food.

Clanworthy, brave Clanworthy,
Clanworthy for aye
Through fire and water brought wine
That Mrs Blow might not die.

Mrs Blow has now become their only thought
And care,
All the other animals

In the forest of Cluny
Say there is no talking to them now
Because their only thought is Mrs Blow.
Hey Hopdance,
How is Mrs Blow?
Oh, very well now.
She is quite recovered, said the dog.

But a woodcutter has opined
It was the spirit of Mrs Blow he saw dancing one night
When a full moon fell on the glade of Cluny
With her animals, and that
Clanworthy and Hopdance
Stood upright upon their hind legs
Holding the hand of Mrs Blow the widow
As if she was a child.
If it was Mrs Blow
But he said he thought it was the ghost
Of Mrs Blow, her spirit; and that
The animals, too, did not look like animals; he said
It was three spirits playing ring-a-ring
With crowns on their head.

So everyone remembered then
That a long time ago
The King and Queen had lost their little children
As
A great witch had changed the boys into animals
And the girl into Mrs Blow the widow

Crying: Hopdance, go Hopdance; Clanworthy go,
For a hundred and seven years
Be the animals of Mrs Blow.

Everyone was glad it had come right
And that the princes and the princess
Were dancing in the night.

Stevie Smith

Timothy Winters

Timothy Winters comes to school
With eyes as wide as a football pool,
Ears like bombs and teeth like splinters:
A blitz of a boy is Timothy Winters.

His belly is white, his neck is dark,
And his hair is an exclamation mark.
His clothes are enough to scare a crow
And through his britches the blue winds blow.

When teacher talks he won't hear a word
And he shoots down dead the arithmetic-bird,
He licks the patterns off his plate
And he's not even heard of the Welfare State.

Timothy Winters has bloody feet
And he lives in a house on Suez Street,
He sleeps in a sack on the kitchen floor
And they say there aren't boys like him any more.

Old Man Winters likes his beer
And his missus ran off with a bombardier,
Grandma sits in the grate with a gin
And Timothy's dosed with an aspirin.

The Welfare Worker lies awake
But the law's as tricky as a ten-foot snake,
So Timothy Winters drinks his cup
And slowly goes on growing up.

At Morning Prayers the Master helves*
For children less fortunate than ourselves,
And the loudest response in the room is when
Timothy Winters roars 'Amen!'

* helves: a dialect word from north Cornwall used to
describe the alarmed lowing of cattle (as when a cow is
separated from her calf); a desperate, pleading note

So come one angel, come on ten:
Timothy Winters says 'Amen
Amen amen amen amen.'
Timothy Winters, Lord.
                          Amen.

Charles Causley

Once upon a time . . .

Once upon a time
There were 500 naked men
Who had a religion called
Love God.
One day they decided to show
God that they loved Him
By making a loud kissing sound.
They would arise simultaneously
From their black polyvinyl
couches at a prearranged signal.
This was made by an atheist
Slamming his fist into a plank
Of 8 by 1 deal.
He did it.
So they rose simultaneously,
Making a loud kissing sound.
God heard it.
It brought Him to his feet,
Surprised but pleased.
As a reward,
He made them
Parthenogenic.
But they were
So embarrassed
That nothing
Ever came of it.

Ivor Cutler

The knee

On earth there roams a lonely knee.
It's just a knee, that's all.
It's not a tent, it's not a tree,
it's just a knee, that's all.

In battle, long ago, a man
was riddled through and through.
The knee alone escaped unhurt
as if it were taboo.

Since then there roams a lonely knee,
it's just a knee, that's all.
It's not a tent, it's not a tree,
it's just a knee, that's all.

Christian Morgenstern

Madam

Madam
I have sold you
an electric plug
an electric torch
an electric blanket
an electric bell
an electric cooker
an electric kettle
an electric fan
an electric iron
an electric drier
an electric mixer
an electric washer
an electric peeler
an electric sweeper
an electric mower
an electric singer
an electric knife
an electric clock
an electric fire
an electric switch
an electric toothbrush
an electric razor
an electric teapot
an electric eye
an electric light.
Allow me to sell you
an electric chair.

Christopher Logue

The last gangster

Waiting by the window
my feet enwrapped with the dead bootleggers of Chicago
I am the last gangster, safe, at last,
waiting by a bullet-proof window.

I look down the street and know
the two torpedoes from St Louis.
I've watched them grow old
. . . guns rusting in their arthritic hands.

Gregory Corso

The Earth-ling

*Countless years ago the people of Alzorus used the
planet Earth as a lunatic asylum. They called the
people they dumped there 'Earth-lings'.*

I am an earth-ling.
My memory goes back a long way.
I was dumped here long ago.
I lived beneath some overhanging rocks.
Around me at night, through the sky's black sheet,
stars poured down.
It was lonely sitting for centuries
beneath that rain-drenched rock,
wrapped in furs, afraid of this whole terrible planet.
I grew fed up with the taste of its food.
I made fire, I slaughtered creatures,
I walked through a forest and made friends.
I copied the things they made.
I walked through another forest and found enemies,
I destroyed the things they made.
I went on and on and on and on,
and on a bit more.
I crossed mountains, I crossed new oceans.
I became familiar with this world.
Time would not stop running when I asked it.
I could not whistle for it to come back.
I invented a couple of languages.
I wrote things down.
I invented books.
Time passed.
My inventions piled up. The natives of this planet feared
    me.
Some tried to destroy me.
Rats came. A great plague swept over the world.
Many of me died.

I am an earth-ling.
I invented cities. I tore them down.
I sat in comfort. I sat in poverty. I sat in boredom.
Home was a planet called Alzorus. A tiny far off star –
One night it went out. It vanished.
I am an earth-ling, exiled for ever from my beginnings.
Time passed. I did things. Time passed. I grew exhausted
One day
A great fire swept the world.
I wanted to go back to the beginning.
It was impossible.
The rock I had squatted under melted.
Friends became dust,
Dust became the only friend.
In the dust I drew faces of people.
I am putting this message on a feather
and puffing it up among the stars.
I have missed so many things out!
But this is the basic story, the terrible story.
I am an earth-ling,
I was dumped here long ago.
Mistakes were made.

Brian Patten

Alternative endings to an unwritten ballad

I stole through the dungeons, while everyone slept,
  Till I came to the cage where the Monster was kept.
There, locked in the arms of a Giant Baboon,
  Rigid and smiling, lay . . . MRS RAVOON!

I climbed the clock-tower in the first morning sun
  And 'twas midday at least ere my journey was done;
But the clock never sounded the last stroke of noon,
  For there, from the clapper, swung MRS RAVOON.

I hauled in the line, and I took my first look
  At the half-eaten horror that hung from the hook.
I had dragged from the depths of the limpid lagoon
  The luminous body of MRS RAVOON.

I fled in the tempest, through lightning and thunder,
  And there, as a flash split the darkness asunder,
Chewing a rat's-tail and mumbling a rune,
  Mad in the moat squatted MRS RAVOON.

I stood by the waters so green and so thick,
  And I stirred at the scum with my old, withered stick;
When there rose through the ooze, like a monstrous balloon,
  The bloated cadaver of MRS RAVOON.

Facing the fens, I looked back from the shore
  Where all had been empty a moment before;
And there, by the light of the Lincolnshire moon,
  Immense on the marshes, stood . . . MRS RAVOON!

Paul Dehn

Mrs Murphy and
Mrs Murphy's kids

Mrs Murphy,
  If you please,
Kept her kids
  In a can of peas.

The kids got bigger,
  And the can filled up,
So she moved them into
  A measuring cup.

But the kids got bigger
  And the cup got crammed,
So she poured them into
  A frying pan.

But the kids grew bigger
  And the pan began to stink,
So she pitched them all
  In the kitchen sink.

But the kids kept growing
  And the sink went *kaplooey*,
So she dumped them on their ears
  In a crate of chop suey.

But the kids kept growing
  And the crate got stuck,
So she carted them away
  In a ten-ton truck.

And she said, 'Thank goodness
  I remembered that truck
Or my poor little children
  Would be out of luck!'

But the darn kids grew
  Till the truck wouldn't fit,
And she had to haul them off
  To a gravel pit.

But the kids kept growing
  Till the pit was too small,
So she bedded them down
  In a shopping mall.

But the kids grew enormous
  And the mall wouldn't do,
So she herded them together
  In an empty zoo.

But the kids grew gigantic
And the fence went *pop*!
So she towed them away
  To a mountain top.

But the kids just grew
  And the mountain broke apart,
And she said, 'Darned kids,
  They were pesky from the start!'

So she waited for a year,
  And she waited for another,
And the kids grew up
  And had babies like their mother.

And Mrs Murphy's kids –
  You can think what you please –
Kept all *their* kids
  In a can of peas.

Dennis Lee

Birdswing

Got a letter
from a thrush.
Come and see
me compose.
So I went.
She stuck
her beak
into the ink
and sputtered
on to the manuscript.
Then sang it.
Tra la la
tweet tweet
warble warble
ptui ptui.
When she finished
I was asked
for an opinion.
With a grave look
I opined:
Well
it's very good.
Regular thrush music
good range
plenty of variety
nice timbre.

Look Cutler
said thrush
do you think
it's worth
making a demodisc
or a tape
and
going round the agents?

I think
it's chart material.
Look thrush
I replied
it could only succeed
as a gimmick.
Yea, I suppose,
she tweeted
and flew
into a stump.

Ivor Cutler

The wild Yorkshire pudding

On moors we are hunting
The wild Yorkshire pudding;
The small ones are nippy,
The fat ones are grunting.

They snuggle together
And hide in the heather;
The young ones are tasty,
The old ones like leather.

We jump on and snatch 'em;
They shriek as we catch 'em;
On cords which take twenty
We string and attach 'em.

They dry them in Batley;
They can them in Ilkley.
You will find they are served
Where menus are stately.

Our terriers are scenting
The rock-crevice-skulking
Tremendous with gravy
And wild Yorkshire pudding.

Alan Dixon

Ballad of the breadman

Mary stood in the kitchen
  Baking a loaf of bread.
An angel flew in through the window.
  'We've a job for you,' he said.

'God in his big gold heaven,
  Sitting in his big blue chair,
Wanted a mother for his little son.
  Suddenly saw you there.'

Mary shook and trembled,
  'It isn't true what you say.'
'Don't say that,' said the angel.
  'The baby's on its way.'

Joseph was in the workshop
  Planing a piece of wood.
'The old man's past it,' the neighbours said.
  'The girl's been up to no good.'

'And who was that elegant fellow,'
  They said, 'in the shiny gear?'
The things they said about Gabriel
  Were hardly fit to hear.

Mary never answered,
  Mary never replied.
She kept the information,
  Like the baby, safe inside.

It was election winter.
  They went to vote in town.
When Mary found her time had come
  The hotels let her down.

The baby was born in an annexe
  Next to the local pub.
At midnight, a delegation
  Turned up from the Farmers' Club.

They talked about an explosion
That made a hole in the sky,
Said they'd been sent to the Lamb & Flag
To see God come down from on high.

A few days later a bishop
And a five-star general were seen
With the head of an African country
In a bullet-proof limousine.

'We've come,' they said, 'with tokens
For the little boy to choose.'
Told the tale about war and peace
In the television news.

After them came the soldiers
With rifle and bomb and gun,
Looking for enemies of the state.
The family had packed and gone.

When they got back to the village
The neighbours said, to a man,
'That boy will never be one of us,
Though he does what he blessed well can.'

He went round to all the people
A paper crown on his head.
Here is some bread from my father.
Take, eat, he said.

Nobody seemed very hungry.
Nobody seemed to care.
Nobody saw the god in himself
Quietly standing there.

He finished up in the papers.
He came to a very bad end.
He was charged with bringing the living to life.
No man was that prisoner's friend.

There's only one kind of punishment
    To fit that kind of a crime.
They rigged a trial and shot him dead.
    They were only just in time.

They lifted the young man by the leg,
    They lifted him by the arm,
They locked him in a cathedral
    In case he came to harm.

They stored him safe as water
    Under seven rocks.
One Sunday morning he burst out
    Like a jack-in-the-box.

Through the town he went walking.
    He showed them the holes in his head.
Now do you want any loaves? he cried.
    'Not today,' they said.

Charles Causley

The fat budgie

I have a little budgie
He is my very pal
I take him walks in Britain
I hope I always shall.

I call my budgie Jeffrey
My grandad's name's the same
I call him after grandad
Who had a feathered brain.

Some people don't like budgies
The little yellow brats
They eat them up for breakfast
Or give them to their cats.

My uncle ate a budgie
It was so fat and fair.
I cried and called him Ronnie
He didn't seem to care

Although his name was Arthur
It didn't mean a thing.
He went into a petshop
And ate up everything.

The doctors looked inside him,
To see what they could do,
But he had been too greedy
He died just like a zoo.

My Jeffrey chirps and twitters
When I walk into the room,
I make him scrambled egg on toast
And feed him with a spoon.

He sings like other budgies
But only when in trim
But most of all on Sunday
That's when I plug him in.

He flies about the room sometimes
And sits upon my bed
And if he's really happy
He does it on my head.

He's on a diet now you know
From eating far too much
They say if he gets fatter
He'll have to wear a crutch.

It would be funny wouldn't it
A budgie on a stick
Imagine all the people
Laughing till they're sick.

So that's my budgie Jeffrey
Fat and yellow too
I love him more than daddie
And I'm only thirty-two.

John Lennon

Thrum

Thrum drew
A small map

He put in
The small countries
The lizards and
The bugs and
The snails and
The worms

He made a mountain
And a green tree
And small rocks
And smaller rocks

He made a river
And a little fish

He made a meadow
And a little mouse

He made specks
That were ants
He made a queer smile
On the countenance of
A bee

He made a person
Small as a
Minnow
He made white birds
In a blue sky
But because he had no
Yellow
He couldn't draw the sun

He made an ocean
And a small boat
He made daytime and
Nightime and a
Small evening star

He signed his name
In small letters
At the bottom
Almost too small
To be able to
See

He loved his small
Map
With its small
Small secrets

Grim came and tore it
Up

Susan Musgrave

Hide and seek

Call out. Call loud: 'I'm ready! Come and find me!'
The sacks in the toolshed smell like the seaside.
They'll never find you in this salty dark,
But be careful that your feet aren't sticking out.
Wiser not to risk another shout.
The floor is cold. They'll probably be searching
The bushes near the swing. Whatever happens
You mustn't sneeze when they come prowling in.
And here they are, whispering at the door;
You've never heard them sound so hushed before.
Don't breathe. Don't move. Stay dumb. Hide in your
  blindness.
They're moving closer, someone stumbles, mutters;
Their words and laughter scuffle, and they're gone.
But don't come out just yet; they'll try the lane
And then the greenhouse and back here again.

They must be thinking that you're very clever,
Getting more puzzled as they search all over.
It seems a long time since they went away.
Your legs are stiff, the cold bites through your coat;
The dark damp smell of sand moves in your throat.
It's time to let them know that you're the winner.
Push off the sacks. Uncurl and stretch. That's better!
Out of the shed and call to them: 'I've won!
Here I am! Come and own up I've caught you!'
The darkening garden watches. Nothing stirs.
The bushes hold their breath; the sun is gone.
Yes, here you are. But where are they who sought you?

Vernon Scannell

A vacation on Earth

Chiefly, it is blue. People use
the old archaic words, which sound
larklike on their tongues,
not on mine. 'I am fine,

thank you.' Or 'Could you direct me
to the Mediterranean Sea?'
I ate an ice cream cone,
and I saw the recent pope.

It is hard to believe
we have our source in this nightmare
tangle of vegetable matter and stone,
that this hell is where

it all began. Yet there is something
in the light or in the air . . .
I don't know what, but it is there.
I never thought I would descend

to such bathos! I did not come to Earth
to dredge up these worthless weary myths.
There was no mother at my birth –
I do not need one now.

Yesterday I visited Italy: Rome,
Florence, Venice, and the famous church
museum. There was little I missed.
But tomorrow, thank god, I go home.

Thomas M. Disch

Exercise book

Two and two four
four and four eight
eight and eight sixteen . . .
Once again! says the master
Two and two four
four and four eight
eight and eight sixteen.
But look! the lyre-bird
high on the wing
the child sees it
the child hears it
the child calls it
Save me
play with me
bird!
So the bird alights
and plays with the child
Two and two four. . . .
Once again! says the master

and the child plays
and the bird plays too. . . .
Four and four eight
eight and eight sixteen
and twice sixteen makes what?
Twice sixteen makes nothing
least of all thirty-two
anyhow
and off they go.
For the child has hidden
the bird in his desk
and all the children
hear its song
and all the children
hear the music
and eight and eight in their turn
off they go
and four and four and two and two
in their turn fade away
and one and one makes neither one nor two
but one by one off they go.
And the lyre-bird sings
and the child sings
and the master shouts
When you've quite finished playing the fool!
But all the children
are listening to the music
and the walls of the classroom
quietly crumble.
The windowpanes turn
once more to sand
the ink is sea
the desk is trees
the chalk is cliffs
and the quill pen
a bird again.

Jacques Prévert

Lo, the ghost of our
least favourite uncle

not exactly a funeral oration

Lo, the ghost of our least favourite Uncle!
For he drank and he fell and he swore.
We could hardly wait up for his death knell,
When it came we said: 'Great! What a bore!'
We could hardly hold breath for his funeral,
And we rushed him pellmell to the green,
And we buried him most uncontritely,
In the fastest performance yet seen.
And we danced a pig-jig in the summer
And we laughed when we thought of next fall
When our mostly unfavourite Uncle
Would not be around us at *all*!
And we drove in a flash and a flurry
In a hurry of motor to town
To celebrate Uncle's entombment
With dandelion wine all around.
But our smiles and our joys were foreshortened
As soon after that burial day
A ghost that resembled our Uncle
Arrived one dark midnight to stay.
My grandma found him in the coal-bin
With his scuppers full up on noon wine,
And my grandpa spied him in the attic
Where the weather of ancient was fine.
And me-myself-I saw him hanging
On a hook in the closet full-length,
And my brother swore Unk was ghost-monkey
Who swarmed the night oak-tree for strength.
At dusk when the old apples rattled
Torn loose by the wind, tossed to roof,
They ran like a caper of ghost-feet
And stomped on the dark earth like hoof.

Whatever the sound, *that* was Uncle,
Whatever the whisper or breath;
If a mouse came for cheese in the pantry
It was a small visit from Death.
Or late nights when the ice dripped from icebox
To fall in the drip-pan below
And our dog lapped the clear snowy waters,
Those sounds were my Uncle, I *know*.
And when wind turned a corner of Nowhere
And leaned on our house for a test,
All those creakings and groanings of timber
Were the death throes of Uncle, unblessed.
So one night I got up with a candle
And crept to the foot of the stair,
And saw huddled there in each shadow
A lurk that old Death had put there.

So I revved up my shouter and screamer
To shake dust from the eaves to the bin
And I yelled: 'Get! Go! Leave with your hauntings!
Go bury yourself, Uncle Sin!'
And the creeps and the shades and the shambles
Gave a shake and a mourn and a yawn
And with moaning, ochoning, lamenting
Ran off down the red crack of dawn.
And the household, aroused in their bedclothes,
Who'd heard this small boychild's uproar,
Sat up with wild smiles and applauded
Or beat their old canes on the floor.
And from that night to this: no more hauntings,
And my family lived just to boast
That a twelve-year-old boy with a loud mouth
Had slaughtered the pale family ghost.

Where my clamour was always a nuisance
And my loudness was always a sin,
I'm now the loud pal, pride, and pleasure
Of my soft-spoken kith and mute kin.

Ray Bradbury

The day the world ended

for John Betjeman

The washing machine was whirling away,
    The cat was licking its tail,
A pile of clothes was on top and done,
    And a pile was below in a pail.

The basement was growing steamy and warm,
    The cat was alert and wise,
The dryer was doing its job quite well,
    And the jeans were rattling their flies.

The regular wash was all clean and dry,
    The *Tide* was back on the sink,
The handkerchiefs were all fresh and smooth,
    And the towels looked bright and pink.

The revolving drum had come to a halt,
    The shirts were all shut inside,
The air was thick with the smell of suds,
    And the cat's eyes were open wide.

The world was travelling round the sun,
    The moon was out in the West,
A spider was tottering over the floor,
    And the maid was wringing a vest.

The hangers were on the clothes horse,
    The socks were dripping and wet,
The cat had gone for a plate of fish,
    And the sun had started to set.

The light was up in the living-room,
    The lamp was down in the hall,
The cat was hunting a brown rat,
    And nothing had happened at all.

George MacBeth

A Shropshire lad

N.B. *This should be recited with a Midland accent. Captain Webb, the swimmer and a relation of Mary Webb by marriage, was born at Dawley in an industrial district in Shropshire.*

The gas was on in the Institute,
  The flare was up in the gym,
A man was running a mineral line,
  A lass was singing a hymn,
When Captain Webb the Dawley man,
  Captain Webb from Dawley,
Came swimming along the old canal
  That carried the bricks to Lawley.
    Swimming along –
    Swimming along –
    Swimming along from Severn,
And paying a call at Dawley Bank while swimming along to Heaven.

The sun shone low on the railway line
  And over the bricks and stacks,
And in at the upstairs windows
  Of the Dawley houses' backs,
When we saw the ghost of Captain Webb,
  Webb in a water sheeting,
Come dripping along in a bathing dress
  To the Saturday evening meeting.
    Dripping along –
    Dripping along –
    To the Congregational Hall;
Dripping and still he rose over the sill and faded away in a wall.

There wasn't a man in Oakengates
    That hadn't got hold of the tale,
And over the valley in Ironbridge,
    And round by Coalbrookdale,
How Captain Webb the Dawley man,
    Captain Webb from Dawley,
Rose rigid and dead from the old canal
    That carries the bricks to Lawley.
        Rigid and dead –
        Rigid and dead –
        To the Saturday congregation,
Paying a call at Dawley Bank on his way to his destination.

John Betjeman

Note: Captain Matthew Webb became famous as the first man to swim the English Channel in 1875.

Parrot

The old sick green parrot
High in a dingy cage
Sick with malevolent rage
Beadily glutted his furious eye
On the old dark
Chimneys of Noel Park

Far from his jungle green
Over the seas he came
To the yellow skies, to the dripping rain,
To the night of his despair.
And the pavements of his street
Are shining beneath the lamp
With a beauty that's not for one
Born under a tropical sun.

He has croup. His feathered chest
Knows no minute of rest.
High on his perch he sits
And coughs and spits,
Waiting for death to come.
Pray heaven it won't be long.

Stevie Smith

On the island of strange mutations

There were six heads,
Identical sextuplets.
The first head wore no make-up, child of nature.
The second head made itself up to the eyes.
The third head was a brunette.
The fourth head tried tints, ash-blonde and auburn.
The fifth head wore a bright smile.
The sixth head had downcast lips.
The first head said, I am tired, I must rest.
The second head said, I am wide awake, I want to dance.
The third head said, Have you a cigarette?
The fourth head said, Lung cancer, I am giving up.
The fifth head said, Never leave me.
The sixth head said, I can't bear being tied down.
Six heads
On a single body, the body of Scylla;
Lovely wrangling heads.
They were forced to yield to each other
Like traffic at an experimental roundabout.
When some felt merely alone, others felt lonely.
When some were stuffing, others were on a diet.
Some wanted a career, others wanted domesticity.
They agreed on one thing only:
Life was all complication and pain,
They longed for harmony and simplicity.
Yet whenever they mentioned this,
The fact that they were in agreement
Produced a terrible boredom and ennui
In Scylla: she had to quarrel with herself again.

D. M. Thomas

Doll poem

A favourite doll
knows the pain of a child's farewell.
Buried in the crib in the attic it dies for ever.
Candy-colours fade
long pants lead us elsewhere
and a child's hands are getting hair.
Chewed-pencils, clips, pennies in our pockets
where are they?
The child's body is longer
long as the earth
everybody walks on him, some on wheelchairs,
long mad envious journey.
Soda and fig-newtons will erupt from the mouth.

Gregory Corso

The weak monk

The monk sat in his den,
He took the mighty pen
And wrote 'Of God and Men.'

One day the thought struck him
It was not according to Catholic doctrine;
His blood ran dim.

He wrote till he was ninety years old,
Then he shut the book with a clasp of gold,
And buried it under the sheep fold.

He'd enjoyed it so much, he loved to plod,
And he thought he'd a right to expect that God
Would rescue his book alive from the sod.

Of course it rotted in the snow and rain;
No one will ever know now what he wrote of God and
    men.
For this the monk is to blame.

Stevie Smith

The river god

(Of the River Mimram in Hertfordshire)

I may be smelly and I may be old,
Rough in my pebbles, reedy in my pools,
But where my fish float by I bless their swimming
And I like the people to bathe in me, especially women.
But I can drown the fools
Who bathe too close to the weir, contrary to rules.
And they take a long time drowning
As I throw them up now and then in a spirit of clowning.
Hi yih, yippity-yap, merrily I flow,
O I may be an old foul river but I have plenty of go.
Once there was a lady who was too bold
She bathed in me by the tall black cliff where the water
    runs cold,
So I brought her down here
To be my beautiful dear.
Oh will she stay with me will she stay
This beautiful lady, or will she go away?
She lies in my beautiful deep river bed with many a weed
To hold her, and many a waving reed.
Oh who would guess that a beautiful white face lies there
Waiting for me to smooth and wash away the fear
She looks at me with. Hi yih, do not let her
Go. There is no one on earth who does not forget her
Now. They say I am a foolish old smelly river
But they do not know of my wide original bed
Where the lady waits, with her golden sleepy head.
If she wishes to go I will not forgive her.

Stevie Smith

from
Aunts and Uncles

When Aunty Flo
Became a Crow
She had a bed put in a tree;
And there she lay
And read all day
Of ornithology.

When Aunty Vi
Became a Fly
Her favourite nephew
Sought her life;
How could he know
That with each blow
He bruised his Uncle's wife?

When Uncle Sam
Became a Ham
We did not care to carve him up;
He struggled so;
We let him go
And gave him to the pup.

Mervyn Peake

George and the dragonfly

Georgie Jennings was spit almighty.
When the golly was good
he could down a dragonfly at 30 feet
and drown a 100 midges with the fallout.
At the drop of a cap
he would outspit lads
years older and twice his size.
Freckled and rather frail
he assumed the quiet dignity
beloved of schoolboy heroes.

But though a legend in his own playtime
Georgie Jennings failed miserably in the classroom
    and left school at 15 to work for his father.
And talents such as spitting
are considered unbefitting
for upandcoming porkbutchers.

I haven't seen him since,
but like to imagine some summer soiree
when, after a day moistening mince,
George and his wife entertain tanned friends.
And after dinner, sherrytongued talk
drifts back to schooldays
The faces halfrecalled, the adventures
overexaggerated. And the next thing
that shy sharpshooter of days gone by
    is led, vainly protesting, on to the lawn
where, in the hush of a golden august evening
a reputation, 20 years tall, is put to the test.
So he takes extra care as yesterheroes must,
fires, and a dragonfly, encapsulated, bites the dust.
Then amidst bravos and tinkled applause,
blushing, Georgie leads them back indoors.

Roger McGough

Five learned Scholars

Five learned Scholars
were each paid a dollar
to see if they could find out something new,
but they met with some resistance
for according to the distance
they noticed things got smaller or they grew.

A ship far out at sea
looked no bigger than a flea
relatively speaking of its size
so they thought it more effective
to eliminate perspective
as all they had to do was close their eyes.

Having thus removed illusion
they were thrown into confusion
for they found the darkness painful to their shins,
so it met with their approval
to order the removal
of everything from elephants to pins.

A passion in them burned,
they left no worm unturned,
they flattened all the bumps to fill in holes,
and from Leicester to East Anglia
made Continents rectangular
and evenly distributed the Poles.

But still it was no use –
from their sponsors came abuse
along with threats of not a penny more,
so in exasperation
they proclaimed imagination
the novelty they'd all been searching for.

So the five of them sat drinking
each alone amongst their thinking
but of the Gab each still had the gift,
and so with each uncorking
the wine did all the talking
and as each one held forth each one came fifth.

And long into the night
They argued wrong and right
'til Death itself called out, 'Last orders please'.
So the five learned scholars
sang a song for five dollars
and left this life upon their hands and knees.

Neil Innes

Leonardo

Leonardo is feeding the jungle.
The jungle is rumble-hungry, full of
lost children.

They eat anything.
They eat fish-gloat and penguin-glut.
They eat toad-frogs and greasy-pig,
oily-snake and beetle-grunt.
They eat one another.

They eat wolf-sly and chicken-slaughter.
They eat everyone.
They eat tourist-fingers and camera-icing,
money-gizzard and aeroplane-lick.

Lost children with teeth for tearing meat.
Little children who gobble their own mothers.
Lost little children chewing loud and hard and fast.
Greedy little creatures!
The horribles!

Susan Musgrave

Whale

A whale lay cast up on the island's shore
  in the shallow water of the outgoing tide.
    He struggled to fill his lungs,
    He grew acquainted with weight.

And the people came and said, Kill it, it is food.
And the witch-doctor said, It is sacred, it must not be
  harmed.
And a girl came and with an empty coconut-shell
  scooped the seawater and let it run over the whale's blue
  bulk.

A small desperate eye showing white all round
  the dark iris. The great head flattened against
    sand as a face pressed against a glass.

And a white man came and said, If all the people
  push we can float it off on the next tide.
And the witch-doctor said, It is taboo, it must not be
  touched.

And the people drifted away.
And the white man cursed and ran off to the next village for
  help.

And the girl stayed.
She stayed as the tide went out.
The whale's breath came in harsh spasms.
Its skin was darkening in the sun.
The girl got children to form a chain
of coconut-shells filled with fresh water
that she poured over his skin.

The whale's eye seemed calmer.

With the high tide the white man came back.

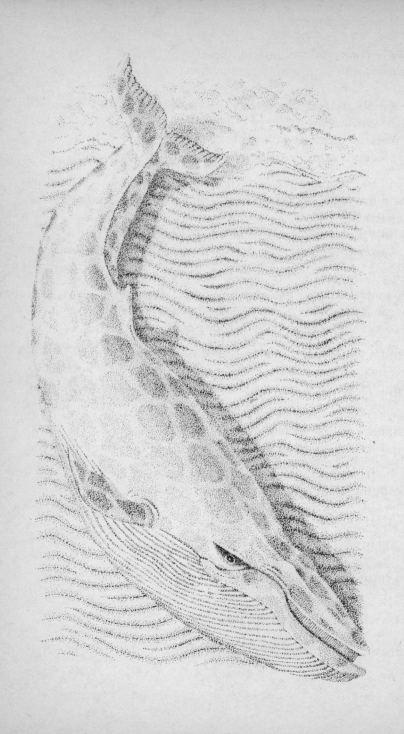

As the whale felt sea reach to his eye he reared
on fins and tail flukes, his spine arced
and he slapped it all down together, a great leap
into the same inert sand.
His eye rolled
in panic as again he lifted and crashed down,
    exhausted, and again lifted and crashed down,
        and again, and again.

The white man couldn't bear his agony and strode away,
    as the tide receded.
He paced and paced the island and cursed God.

Now the whale didn't move.
The girl stroked his head
and as the moon came up
she sang to him
of friends long dead and children grown and gone,
sang like a mother to the whale,

and sang of unrequited love.

And later in the night
    when his breaths had almost lost touch
        she leant her shoulder against his cheek

and told him stories, with many details,
of the mud-skipping fish that lived
        in the mangroves on the lagoon.

Her voice
and its coaxing pauses
was as if fins
were bearing him up to the surface of the ocean
to breathe and see,
as with a clot of blood falling on her brow
the whale passed clear from the body of his death.

(after an incident in Lyall Watson's *Gifts of Unknown Things*)

D. M. Thomas

The castaways or vote for Caliban

The Pacific Ocean –
A blue demi-globe.
Islands like punctuation marks.

A cruising airliner,
Passengers unwrapping pats of butter.
A hurricane arises,
Tosses the plane into the sea.

Five of them, flung on to an island beach,
Survived.
Tom the reporter.
Susan the botanist.
Jim the high-jump champion.
Bill the carpenter.
Mary the eccentric widow.

Tom the reporter sniffed out a stream of drinkable water.
Susan the botanist identified a banana tree.
Jim the high-jump champion jumped up and down and
    gave them each a bunch.
Bill the carpenter knocked up a table for their banana
    supper.
Mary the eccentric widow buried the banana skins,
But only after they had asked her twice.
They all gathered sticks and lit a fire.
There was an incredible sunset.

Next morning they held a committee meeting.
Tom, Susan, Jim and Bill
Voted to make the best of things.
Mary, the eccentric widow, abstained.

Tom the reporter killed several dozen wild pigs.
He tanned their skins into parchment
And printed the *Island News* with the ink of squids.

Susan the botanist developed new strains of banana
Which tasted of chocolate, beefsteak, peanut butter,
Chicken and bootpolish.

Jim the high-jump champion organized organized games
Which he always won easily.

Bill the carpenter constructed a wooden water wheel
And converted the water's energy into electricity.
Using iron ore from the hills, he constructed lampposts.

They all worried about Mary, the eccentric widow,
Her lack of confidence and her –
But there wasn't time to coddle her.

The volcano erupted, but they dug a trench
And diverted the lava into the sea
Where it formed a spectacular pier.
They were attacked by pirates but defeated them
With bamboo bazookas firing
Sea-urchins packed with home-made nitro-glycerine.
They gave the cannibals a dose of their own medicine
And survived an earthquake thanks to their skill in
    jumping.

Tom had been a court reporter
So he became the magistrate and solved disputes.
Susan the Botanist established
A university which also served as a museum.

Jim the high-jump champion
Was put in charge of law-enforcement –
Jumped on them when they were bad.
Bill the carpenter built himself a church,
Preached there every Sunday.
But Mary the eccentric widow . . .
Each evening she wandered down the island's main street,
Past the Stock Exchange, the Houses of Parliament,
The prison and the arsenal.

Past the Prospero Souvenir Shop,
Past the Robert Louis Stevenson Movie Studios,
Past the Daniel Defoe Motel
She nervously wandered and sat on the end of the pier of
    lava,
Breathing heavily.
As if at a loss,
As if at a lover,
She opened her eyes wide
To the usual incredible sunset.

Adrian Mitchell

The dragonfly

There was once a terrible monster
lived in a pond, deep under the water.

Brown as mud he was, in the mud he hid,
among murk of reed-roots, sodden twigs,
with his long hungry belly,
six legs for creeping,
eyes like headlights
awake or sleeping;
but he was not big.

A tiddler came to sneer and jeer
and flaunt his flashing tail –
Ugly old stick-in-the-mud
couldn't catch a snail!
I'm not scared –
when, like a shot,
two pincers nab him, and he's got!

For the monster's jaw hides a clawed stalk
like the arm of a robot, a dinner fork,
that's tucked away cunningly till the last minute –
shoots out – and back with a victim in it!

Days, weeks, months, two years and beyond,
fear of the monster beset the pond;
he lurked, grabbed, grappled, gobbled and grew,
ambushing always somewhere new –

Who saw him last? Does anyone know?
Don't go near the mud! But I must go!
Keep well away from the rushes! But how?
Has anyone seen my brother? Not for a week now –
he's been eaten
for certain!

And then, one day, it was June, they all saw him.
He was coming slowly up out of the mud,
they stopped swimming. No one dared
approach, attack. They kept back.

Up a tall reed they saw him climbing
higher and higher, until
he broke the surface, climbing still.

There he stopped, in the wind and the setting sun.
We're safe at last! they cried. *He's gone!*
What became of the monster, was he ill, was he sad?
Was nobody sorry? Had he crept off to die? Was he mad?

Not one of them saw how, suddenly,
as if an invisible knife had touched his back,
he has split, split completely –
his head split like a lid!
The cage is open. Slowly he comes through,
an emperor, with great eyes burning blue.

91

He rests there, veils of silver a cloak for him.
Night and the little stars travel the black pond,
and now, first light of the day,
his shining cloak wide wings, a flash, a whirr,
a jewelled helicopter,
he's away!

O fully he had served his time,
shunned and unlovely in the drab slime,
for freedom at the end – for the sky –
dazzling hunter, Dragonfly!

Libby Houston

Spacepoem 3: Off course

the golden flood   the weightless seat
the cabin song   the pitch black
the growing beard   the floating crumb
the shining rendezvous   the orbit wisecrack
the hot spacesuit   the smuggled mouth-organ
the imaginary somersault   the visionary sunrise
the turning continents   the space debris
the golden lifeline   the space walk
the crawling deltas   the camera moon
the pitch velvet   the rough sleep
the crackling headphone   the space silence
the turning earth   the lifeline continents
the cabin sunrise   the hot flood
the shining spacesuit   the growing moon
  the crackling somersault   the smuggled orbit
  the rough moon   the visionary rendezvous
  the weightless headphone   the cabin debris
  the floating lifeline   the pitch sleep
  the crawling camera   the turning silence
  the space crumb   the crackling beard
  the orbit mouth-organ   the floating song

Edwin Morgan

The invisible backwards-facing grocer who rose to fame

John Green the grocer lived a hesitant life –
He kept his mother to feed and protect him –
And he would not dare to look for a wife
For he dreaded that women would all reject him;
One spring as football was changing to cricket
And the roar of the traffic was drowned by birds
As he went to buy his springtime season ticket
At the booking office window he read these words:

Don't try to peer through the holes in the glass,
Speak at the opaque space provided.

He caught his diesel with a thoughtful air
And saw the little schoolgirls dressed in black
Crushed up on the front seat combing their hair
In the massive shadow of the driver's back.
And he thought: when those girls see my face
They giggle with a feminine tinkling sound;
I will buy a sheet of glass with an opaque space
And serve in the shop with my back turned round, saying:

Don't try to peer through the holes in the glass,
Speak at the opaque space provided.

The very next day the customers saw
The space above the counter taken
By a sheet of glass not there before;
There was no reply when they asked for bacon.
One of the regulars peered wide-eyed
But all she could see was the back of a head;
Then a hand edged out with her bacon tied
And a neatly printed card which read:

Don't try to peer through the holes in the glass,
Speak at the opaque space provided.

The customers talked, the press came too
They peered and wrote but they couldn't get closer
And soon the whole wondering public knew
Its invisible backwards-facing grocer
His gentlemanly ability to hide all feeling
Made the breasts of the League of Political Women stir;
And so John Green rose via MP for Ealing
To invisible backwards-facing prime minister:
Saying in Parliament and on television and
Sometimes quietly to himself:

Don't try to peer through the holes in the glass,
Speak at the opaque space provided.

Alasdair Clayre

The lovepet

Was it an animal was it a bird?
She stroked it. He spoke to it softly.
She made her voice its happy forest.
He brought it out with sugarlump smiles.
Soon it was licking their kisses.

She gave it the strings of her voice which it swallowed
He gave it the blood of his face it grew eager
She gave it the liquorice of her mouth it began to thrive
He opened the aniseed of his future
And it bit and gulped, grew vicious, snatched
The focus of his eyes
She gave it the steadiness of her hand
He gave it the strength of his spine it ate everything

It began to cry what could they give it
They gave it their calendars it bolted their diaries
They gave it their sleep it gobbled their dreams
Even while they slept
It ate their bodyskin and the muscle beneath
They gave it vows its teeth clashed its starvation
Through every word they uttered

It found snakes under the floor it ate them
It found a spider horror
In their palms and ate it

They gave it double smiles and blank silence
It chewed holes in their carpets
They gave it logic
It ate the colour of their hair
They gave it every argument that would come
They gave it shouting and yelling they meant it
It ate the faces of their children

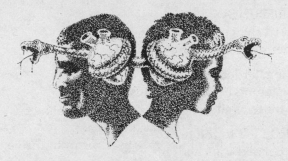

They gave it their photograph albums they gave it their
  records
It ate the colour of the sun
They gave it a thousand letters they gave it money
It ate their future complete it waited for them
Starting and starving
They gave it screams it had gone too far
It ate into their brains
It ate the roof
It ate lonely stone it ate wind crying famine
It went furiously off

They wept they called it back it could have everything
It stripped out their nerves chewed chewed flavourless
It bit at their numb bodies they did not resist
It bit into their blank brains they hardly knew

It moved bellowing
Through a ruin of starlight and crockery

It drew slowly off they could not move

It went far away they could not speak

Ted Hughes

Pantomime poem

'HE'S BEHIND YER!'
chorused the children
but the warning came too late.

The monster leaped forward
and fastening its teeth into his neck,
tore off the head.

The body fell to the floor
'MORE' cried the children

'MORE, MORE, MORE

MORE

MORE

Roger McGough

Napoleon

Children, when was
Napoleon Bonaparte born,
asks teacher.

A thousand years ago, the children say.
A hundred years ago, the children say.
Last year, the children say.
No one knows.

Children, what did
Napoleon Bonaparte do,
asks teacher.

Won a war, the children say.
Lost a war, the children say.
No one knows.

Our butcher had a dog
called Napoleon,
says František.
The butcher used to beat him and the dog died
of hunger
a year ago.

And all the children are now sorry
for Napoleon.

Miroslav Holub

Lizzy's lion

Lizzy had a lion
  With a big, bad roar,
And she kept him in the bedroom
  By the closet-cupboard door;

Lizzy's lion wasn't friendly,
  Lizzy's lion wasn't tame –
Not unless you learned to call him
  By his Secret Lion Name.

One dark night, a rotten robber
  With a rotten robber mask
Snuck in through the bedroom window –
  And he didn't even ask.

And he brought a bag of candy
  That was sticky-icky-sweet,
Just to make friends with a lion
  (If a lion he should meet).

First he sprinkled candy forwards,
  Then he sprinkled candy back;
Then he picked up Lizzy's piggy-bank
  And stuck it in his sack.

But as the rotten robber
  Was preparing to depart,
Good old Lizzy's lion wakened
  With a snuffle and a start.

And he muttered, 'Candy? – piffle!'
  And he rumbled, 'Candy? – pooh!'
And he gave the rotten robber
  An experimental chew.

Then the robber shooed the lion,
    Using every name he knew;
But each time he shooed, the lion
    Merely took another chew.

It was: 'Down, Fido! Leave, Leo!
    Shoo, you good old boy!'
But the lion went on munching
    With a look of simple joy.

It was: 'Stop, Mopsy! Scram, Sambo!
    This is a disgrace!'
But the lion went on lunching
    With a smile upon his face.

Then old Lizzy heard the rumble,
    And old Lizzy heard the fight,
And old Lizzy got her slippers
    And turned on the bedroom light.

There was robber on the toy-shelf!
    There was robber on the rug!
There was robber in the lion
    (Who was looking rather smug)!

But old Lizzy wasn't angry,
    And old Lizzy wasn't rough.
She simply said the Secret Name:
    'Lion! – that's enough.'

Then old Lizzy and her Lion
    Took the toes & tum & head,
And they put them in the garbage,
    And they both went back to bed.

Dennis Lee

Letters from an Irishman to a Rat

Dear Rat:
Never until this moment have I met
a so appreciative guest.
Please God, a diet of my old potatoes
does not reduce your sheen.

Dear Rat:
Forgive my carelessness.
The note I left (correlative potatoes)
was placed too high.
Of course you could not read it.

Dear Rat:
I fear the worst.
My three disgusting children have acquired
a vicious and emaciated dog.
Suppose it heard your name? –
which is forever on their lips.

Dear Rat:
Greatly to my regret I am not rich.
But have you met my neighbour?
A cloudless squire with six pink children, all
animal mad and more intelligent than mine.
And should you live in his house, dearest Rat,
eight Christians (if we include his wife)
would mention you each evening in their prayers,
whereas at my place there are only five.

Christopher Logue

Bedtime story

Long long ago when the world was a wild place
Planted with bushes and peopled by apes, our
Mission Brigade was at work in the jungle.
    Hard by the Congo

Once, when a foraging detail was active
Scouting for greenfly, it came on a grey man, the
Last living man, in the branch of a baobab
    Stalking a monkey.

Earlier men had disposed of, for pleasure,
Creatures whose names we scarcely remember –
Zebra, rhinoceros, elephants, wart-hog,
    Lion, rats, deer. But

After the wars had extinguished the cities
Only the wild ones were left, half-naked
Near the Equator: and here was the last one,
    Starved for a monkey.

By then the Mission Brigade had encountered
Hundreds of such men: and their procedure,
History tells us, was only to feed them:
    Find them and feed them;

Those were the orders. And this was the last one.
Nobody knew that he was, but he was. Mud
Caked on his flat grey flanks. He was crouched, half-
    armed with a shaved spear

Glinting beneath broad leaves. When their jaws cut
Swathes through the bark and he saw fine teeth shine,
Round eyes roll round and forked arms waver
    Huge as the rough trunks

Over his head, he was frightened. Our workers
Marched through the Congo before he was born, but
This was the first time perhaps that he'd seen one.
  Staring in hot, still

Silence, he crouched there: then jumped. With a long swing
Down from his branch, he had angled his spear too
Quickly, before they could hold him, and hurled it
  Hard at the soldier

Leading the detail. How could he know Queen's
Orders were only to help him? The soldier
Winced when the tipped spear pricked him. Unsheathing
  his
  Sting was a reflex.

Later the Queen was informed. There were no more
Men. An impetuous soldier had killed off,
Purely by chance, the penultimate primate.
  When she was certain,

Squadrons of workers were fanned through the Congo
Detailed to bring back the man's picked bones to be
sealed in the archives in amber. I'm quite sure
  Nobody found them

After the most industrious search, though.
Where had the bones gone? Over the earth, dear,
Ground by the teeth of the termites, blown by the
  Wind, like the dodo's.

George MacBeth

The man-moth*

Here, above,
cracks in the buildings are filled with battered moonlight.
The whole shadow of Man is only as big as his hat.
It lies at his feet like a circle for a doll to stand on,
and he makes an inverted pin, the point magnetized to the
  moon.
He does not see the moon; he observes only her vast
  properties,
feeling the queer light on his hands, neither warm nor cold,
of a temperature impossible to record in thermometers.

But when the Man-Moth
pays his rare, although occasional, visits to the surface,
the moon looks rather different to him. He emerges
from an opening under the edge of one of the sidewalks
and nervously begins to scale the faces of the buildings.
He thinks the moon is a small hole at the top of the sky,
proving the sky quite useless for protection.
He trembles, but must investigate as high as he can climb.

Up the façades,
his shadow dragging like a photographer's cloth behind
  him,
he climbs fearfully, thinking that this time he will manage
to push his small head through that round clean opening
and be forced through, as from a tube, in black scrolls on
  the light.
(Man, standing below him, has no such illusions.)
But what the Man-Moth fears most he must do, although
he fails, of course, and falls back scared but quite unhurt.

*Newspaper misprint for 'mammoth'.

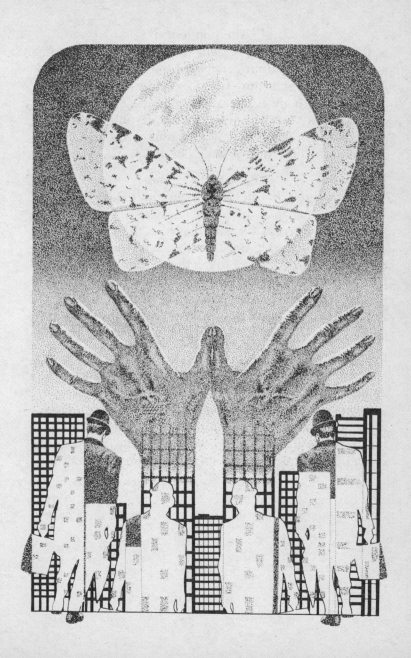

Then he returns
to the pale subways of cement he calls his home. He flits,
he flutters, and cannot get aboard the silent trains
fast enough to suit him. The doors close swiftly.
The Man-Moth always seats himself facing the wrong way
and the train starts at once at its full, terrible speed
without a shift in gears or a gradation of any sort.
He cannot tell the rate at which he travels backwards.

Each night he must
be carried through artificial tunnels and dream recurrent
    dreams.
Just as the ties recur beneath his train, these underlie
his rushing brain. He does not dare look out the window,
for the third rail, the unbroken draught of poison,
runs there beside him. He regards it as a disease
he has inherited the susceptibility to. He has to keep
his hands in his pockets, as others must wear mufflers.

If you catch him,
hold up a flashlight to his eye. It's all dark pupil,
an entire night itself, whose haired horizon tightens
as he stares back, and closes up the eye. Then from the lids
one tear, his only possession; like the bee's sting, slips.
Slyly he palms it, and if you're not paying attention
he'll swallow it. However, if you watch, he'll hand it over,
cool as from underground springs and pure enough to
    drink.

Elizabeth Bishop

The fate of the Supermarket manager

There once was a Supermarket manager
And a very happy manager was he.

He *reduced the prices*
Of the lollies and the ices!
He made *huge cuts*
On the fruit and nuts!
Corn-flakes, steaks
And home-bake cakes,
Dog-food, detergent,
Devil-fish, dates,
He sold at *half*
The market rates!
And (so my sister
Said to me)
He put stickers
On the knickers
In the Lingerie
Saying:
Prices down
By 15p!
And he wrote, as a treat,
By the luncheon meat:
YOU'D HAVE TO BE BARMY
TO BUY THIS SALAMI
So he gave it away
For free!

Yes, there once was a Supermarket manager
And a very happy manager was he.

What a bloke!

He was much admired.

The shop went broke.

He was fired.

Kit Wright

In the land of punctuation

The peaceful land of punctuation
a state of civil strife bemoans:

The dots and commas of the nation
have called the semicolons 'drones'.

They form at once for their intrigue
an antisemicolon league.

The question marks believe it smart
(as always) calmly to depart.

The semicolons with chagrin
lament, as brackets fence them in;

and furthermore one places these
poor prisoners in parentheses.

The minus sign, who then arrives,
takes – swish! – away the captives' lives.

The question marks on their return
look at the bodies with concern.

But, woe, a new war has begun:
The dashes at the commas run

and cut across the latters' necks,
until the overpowered wrecks

(the dashes' minds are murder-bound!)
as semicolons hit the ground.

Both semicolon types they carry
in silence to the cemetarry.

The dashes who survived the war
slink after in the mourning corps.

With colon's aid, the exclamation
mark loudly mourns the victims' lot.

Then, free from comma-like formation,
they all stamp home, dash, dot, dash, dot . . .

Christian Morgenstern

A small dragon

I've found a small dragon in the woodshed.
Think it must have come from deep inside a forest
because it's damp and green and leaves
are still reflecting in its eyes.

I fed it on many things, tried grass,
the roots of stars, hazelnut and dandelion,
but it stared up at me as if to say, I need
food you can't provide.

It made a nest among the coal,
not unlike a bird's but larger,
it's out of place here
and is quite silent.

If you believed in it I would come
hurrying to your house to let you share my wonder,
but I want instead to see
if you yourself will pass this way.

Brian Patten

The Forest of Tangle

Deep in the Forest of Tangle
The King of the Makers sat
With a faggot of stripes for the tiger
And a flitter of wings for the bat.

He'd teeth and he'd claws for the cayman
And barks for the foxes and seals,
He'd a grindstone for sharpening swordfish
And electrical charges for eels.

He'd hundreds of kangaroo-pouches
On bushes and creepers and vines,
He'd hoots for the owls, and for glow-worms
He'd goodness knows how many shines.

He'd bellows for bullfrogs in dozens
And rattles for snakes by the score,
He'd hums for the humming-birds, buzzes for bees,
And elephant trumpets galore.

He'd pectoral fins for sea-fishes
With which they might glide through the air,
He'd porcupine quills and a bevy of bills
And various furs for the bear.

But O the old King of the Makers
With tears could have filled up a bay,
For no one had come to his warehouse
These many long years and a day.

And sadly the King of the Makers
His bits and his pieces he eyed
As he sat on a rock in the midst of his stock
And he cried and he cried and he cried.
He cried and he cried and he cried and he cried,
He cried and he cried and he cried.

Charles Causley

The hurdy-gurdy

I play the piano
said one
I play the fiddle
another
I the banjo I the harp
I the clarinet
I the bagpipe I the flute
and I the flageolet
And they all began to talk talk
talk of what they played.
Nobody heard the music
for the talk talk talk talk
talk, and nobody played
but in a corner a man sat silent:
'What do you play, good sir,' they said,
'who sit so silently
with nothing at all to say?'
'I play the hurdy-gurdy
the knife I also play,'
said the man who sat so silently
with nothing at all to say
and he advanced with knife in hand
and solemnly killed the entire band
and he played the hurdy-gurdy
and his music was so true
so pretty and so new
that the master's little girl came out
from under the piano stool
shaking a sleepy head
and said:
I played at hoop and hide-and-seek
at hopscotch too I played

and once I played with a bucket
and once I played with a spade
I played at being papa, mama,
Puss-in-the-corner and He
I played with a doll and a parasol
and whoever would play with me
I played with my little sister
I played with my little brother
I played at being a policeman
I played at being a robber
But that's all over and done done done
I want to play at murder
that's all over and done I want
to play the hurdy-gurdy
He took the little girl by the hand
and both went on ahead
through town and house and garden
and struck the people dead.
Whereafter they were wed
and they bore a great many children
but
the eldest learnt the piano
the second the violin
the third learnt the bagpipe
the fourth the clarinet
the fifth the flageolet
and they began to talk talk
talk talk and then
nobody heard the music
and all began again!

Jacques Prévert

Funny sort of bloke

Have you heard the latest scandal
About 80-year-old Mr Brown?
He stole from Matron's handbag
Then hitchhiked into town.

Had a slap-up meal at the Wimpy
Then went to a film matinée
One of them sexy blue ones
We're not supposed to see.

Then he bought some jeans and a toupée
Spent the night in a pub
Then carried on till the early hours
Dancing in a club.

They caught him in the morning
Trying to board the London train
He tried to fight them off
But he's back here once again.

They asked him if he'd be a good boy
He said he'd rather not
So they gave him a nice injection
And tied him up in his cot.

He died that very night
Apparently a stroke.
Kept screaming: 'Come out Death and fight.'
Funny sort of bloke.

Roger McGough

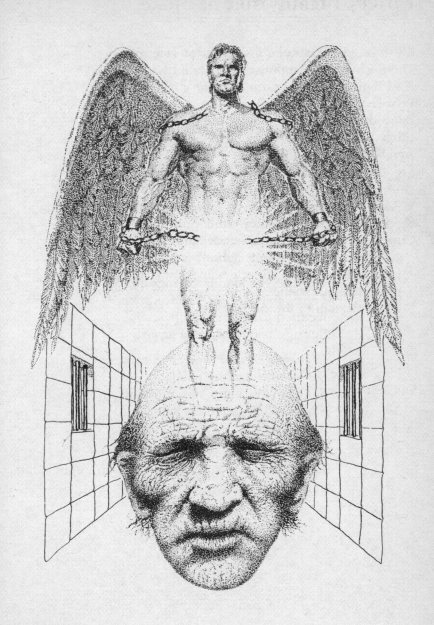

I tried, I really tried

Mesh-faced loudspeakers outshouted Fleet Street,
Their echoes overlapping down Shoe Lane
And Bouverie Street, pronouncing:
WASH YOURSELF POET.
Blurred black police cars from the BBC
Circled me blaring: WASH YOURSELF POET
AND DON'T FORGET YOUR NAVEL.
My ears were clogged with savoury gold wax
And so I failed WASH to hear at first WASH
WASH WASH YOURSELF
Since I was naked and they wore
Chrome-armoured cars and under the cars man-made fibre
    suits and under the suits Y-front pants and under the
    pants official groin protectors and under the groin
    protectors automatics,
I obediently ran to the city's pride,

The Thames, that Lord Mayor's Procession of mercury,
And jumped from Westminster Bridge.
Among half-human mud I bathed
Using a dead cat for a loofah,
Detergent foam for gargle.
I dived, heard the power station's rumble and the moan of
   sewers.
The bubbles of my breath exploded along the waterskin.
Helmeted in dead newspapers, I sprang
Into the petrol-flavoured air
And Big Ben, like a speak-your-weight machine
Intoned WATCH YOURSELF POET.
Clothed in the muck of London, I yelled back:
I HAVE BEEN WASHED IN THE BLOOD OF THE
   THAMES, BIG BROTHER,
AND FROM NOW ON I SHALL USE NO OTHER.

Adrian Mitchell

The chewing-gum song

'Dear friends, we surely all agree
There's almost nothing worse to see
Than some repulsive little bum
Who's always chewing chewing-gum.
(It's very near as bad as those
Who sit around and pick the nose.)
So please believe us when we say
That chewing gum will never pay;
This sticky habit's bound to send
The chewer to a sticky end.
Did any of you ever know
A person called Miss Bigelow?
This dreadful woman saw no wrong
In chewing, chewing all day long.
She chewed while bathing in the tub,
She chewed while dancing at her club,
She chewed in church and on the bus;
It really was quite ludicrous!
And when she couldn't find her gum,
She'd chew up the linoleum,
Or anything that happened near –
A pair of boots, the postman's ear,
Or other people's underclothes,
And once she chewed her boy friend's nose.
She went on chewing till, at last,
Her chewing muscles grew so vast
That from her face her giant chin
Stuck out just like a violin.
For years and years she chewed away,
Consuming fifty bits a day,
Until one summer's eve, alas,
A horrid business came to pass.
Miss Bigelow went late to bed,
For half an hour she lay and read,

Chewing and chewing all the while

Like some great clockwork crocodile.
At last, she put her gum away
Upon a special little tray,
And settled back and went to sleep –
(She managed this by counting sheep).
But now, how strange! Although she slept,
Those massive jaws of her still kept
On chewing, chewing through the night,
Even with nothing there to bite.
They were, you see, in such a groove
They positively *had* to move.
And very grim it was to hear
In pitchy darkness, loud and clear,
This sleeping woman's great big trap
Opening and shutting, *snap-snap-snap*!
Faster and faster, *chop-chop-chop*,
The noise went on, it wouldn't stop.
Until at last her jaws decide
To pause and open extra wide,
And with the most *tremendous* chew
They bit the lady's tongue in two.
Thereafter, just from chewing gum,
Miss Bigelow was always dumb,
And spent her life shut up in some
Disgusting sanatorium.
And *that* is why we'll try so hard
To save Miss Violet Beauregarde
From suffering an equal fate.
She's still quite young. It's not too late,
Provided she survives the cure.
We hope she does. We can't be sure!

Roald Dahl

Understand yourself

Each day, deep in his University,
a scholar shouted: Master!
and answered himself: Yes, Sir?
Then shouted out: Work harder!
and answered: Yes, Sir . . .
And after: Do not be fooled by others!
Answering: Yes, Sir. Yes, Sir.

Christopher Logue

Little Johnny's confession

This morning
   being rather young and foolish
   I borrowed a machinegun my father
   had left hidden since the war, went out,
   and eliminated a number of small enemies.
   Since then I have not returned home.

This morning
   swarms of police with trackerdogs
   wander about the city
   with my description printed
   on their minds, asking:
   'Have you seen him?
   He is seven years old,
   likes Pluto, Mighty Mouse
   and Biffo the Bear,
   have you seen him, anywhere?'

This morning
   sitting alone in a strange playground
   muttering you've blundered, you've blundered
   over and over to myself
   I work out my next move
   but cannot move.
   The trackerdogs will sniff me out,
   they have my lollypops.

Brian Patten

Fish

Fish
are not
very bright
not
by my
standards.
They
never had any
reason to grow
brains. For
one thing
it's hard
to read
under water and
the paper gets too wet
to handle and
there isn't the light and
fins let books slip and you'd
have to hold the
pen in your mouth.

People
who say
'A school of fish'
are
taking
advantage of
their limited
intelligence to poke cruel
fun.

You let
fish be.

Or eat them.

Ivor Cutler

The fish

I caught a tremendous fish
and held him beside the boat
half out of water, with my hook
fast in a corner of his mouth.
He didn't fight.
He hadn't fought at all.
He hung a grunting weight,
battered and venerable
and homely. Here and there
his brown skin hung in strips
like ancient wall-paper,
and its pattern of darker brown
was like wall-paper:
shapes like full-blown roses
stained and lost through age.
He was speckled with barnacles,
fine rosettes of lime,
and infested
with tiny white sea-lice,
and underneath two or three
rags of green weed hung down.
While his gills were breathing in
the terrible oxygen
– the frightening gills,
fresh and crisp with blood,

that can cut so badly –
I thought of the coarse white flesh
packed in like feathers,
the big bones and the little bones,
the dramatic reds and blacks
of his shiny entrails,
and the pink swim-bladder
like a big peony.
I looked into his eyes
which were far larger than mine
but shallower, and yellowed,
the irises backed and packed
with tarnished tinfoil
seen through the lenses
of old scratched isinglass.
They shifted a little, but not
to return my stare.
– It was more like the tipping
of an object towards the light.
I admired his sullen face,
the mechanism of his jaw,
and then I saw
that from his lower lip
– if you could call it a lip –
grim, wet, and weapon-like,

hung five old pieces of fish-line,
or four and a wire leader
with the swivel still attached,
with all their five big hooks
grown firmly in his mouth.
A green line, frayed at the end
where he broke it, two heavier lines,
and a fine black thread
still crimped from the strain and snap
when it broke and he got away.
Like medals with their ribbons
frayed and wavering,
a five-haired beard of wisdom
trailing from his aching jaw.
I stared and stared
and victory filled up
the little rented boat,
from the pool of bilge
where oil had spread a rainbow
around the rusted engine
to the bailer rusted orange,
the sun-cracked thwarts,
the oarlocks on their strings,
the gunnels – until everything
was rainbow, rainbow, rainbow!
And I let the fish go.

Elizabeth Bishop

My brother dreams of giants

My brother dreams the world is the size of a football
  (It is kicked away by a giant.)
He dreams the sky is a large window
  (The giant's child breaks it with a stone.)
He dreams he cannot hear his friends talking
  (Beyond the clouds, the giant's dog is barking.)
He dreams there are no apples in any orchard in the world
  (The giant's wife has picked them all.)
He dreams about the giant's family. He asks,
  'Where do they live?'
'There are no giants,' says father.
'They've gone,' says mother.
My brother will not believe them.

He has seen the sky crack open.
He has heard the giant shouting.

'Where do the giants live!' he yells,
'Where do they live!'
'Is it beyond the sky? I know giants don't die!'

Bernard Logan

Scorflufus

By a well-known
National Health Victim
No. 3908631

There are many diseases,
That strike people's kneeses,
Scorflufus! is one by name
It comes from the East
Packed in bladders of yeast
So the Chinese must take half the blame.

There's a case in the files
Of Sir Barrington-Pyles
While hunting a fox one day
Shot up in the air
And *remained hanging there!*
While the hairs on his socks turned grey!

Aye! Scorflufus had struck!
At man, beast and duck.
And the knees of the world went Bong!
Some knees went Ping!
Other knees turned to string
From Balham to old Hong-Kong.

Should you hold your life dear,
Then the remedy's clear,
If you're offered some yeast – don't eat it!
Turn the offer down flat –
Don your travelling hat –
Put an egg in your boot – and beat it!

Spike Milligan

On a portrait of a deaf man

The kind old face, the egg-shaped head,
   The tie, discreetly loud,
The loosely fitting shooting clothes,
A closely fitting shroud.

He liked old City dining-rooms,
   Potatoes in their skin,
But now his mouth is wide to let
   The London clay come in.

He took me on long silent walks
   In country lanes when young,
He knew the name of ev'ry bird
   But not the song it sung.

And when he could not hear me speak
   He smiled and looked so wise
That now I do not like to think
   Of maggots in his eyes.

He liked the rain-washed Cornish air
   And smell of ploughed-up soil,
He liked a landscape big and bare
   And painted it in oil.

But least of all he liked that place
   Which hangs on Highgate Hill
Of soaked Carrara-covered earth
   For Londoners to fill.

He would have liked to say good-bye,
   Shake hands with many friends,
In Highgate now his finger-bones
   Stick through his finger-ends.

You, God, who treat him thus and thus,
   Say 'Save his soul and pray.'
You ask me to believe You and
   I only see decay.

John Betjeman

The kitchen girl's task

A demon took over Frank, chief
   at the café on the motorway:
arms akimbo, as midnight clicks, he
   summons one of the girls, says:

I want you to count the tealeaves
   we've used here today,
and I'll wait for the right answer.

The prince could not wait, he left her.
   Tears and the fumes of the bins
had sympathy from the clouds of morning.

The prince set out to find his enemies
   who would not wait for man or beast.
Regularly he wrote her letters,
   repeating her unchanging name.

One night, in a dream, she saw
   the little sodden leaves rise,
rank themselves in rows of ten.

She read his considerate lines:
  'How bright I remember your eyes
in all that dry glare.'

'Today we picked up the scent again.'
  'I've found true friends here!'
'We're having *Freedom*
  tattooed on our right wrists.'

Sometimes she put down cloth or knife
  to wander within the boundary.
She would not have heard Rumpelstiltskin
  if he had shouted in her ear.

Silence for her became a rule;
  she was ashamed – and Frank was there
ordering her to wipe the stoves
  and wash the floor as usual.

After a while it came to her
  that no two leaves were identical.

Libby Houston

The reason for skylarks

It was nearly morning when the giant
Reached the tree of children.
Their faces shone like white apples
On the cold dark branches
And their dresses and little coats
Made sodden gestures in the wind.
He did not laugh or weep or stamp
His heavy feet. He set to work at once
Lifting them tenderly down
Into a straw basket which was fixed
By a golden strap to his shoulder.
Only one did he drop – a soft pretty child
Whose hair was the colour of watered milk.
She fell into the long grass
And he could not find her
Though he searched until his fingers
Bled and the full light came.

He shook his fist at the sky and called
God a bitter name.

But no answer was made and the giant
Got down on his knees before the tree
And putting his hands about the trunk
Shook
Until all the children had fallen
Into the grass. Then he pranced and stamped
Them to jelly. And still he felt no peace.
He took his half-full basket and set it afire,
Holding it by the handle until
Everything had been burned. He saw now
Two men on steaming horses approaching
From the direction of the world.
And taking a little silver flute
Out of his pocket he played tune
After tune until they came up to him.

Kenneth Patchen

A knock at the door

You open the door
And you step back
From a sheltering bulk. A tumblesky wet January
Mid-morning. Close, tall, in-leaning
Hairiness of a creature, darkness of a person –

A bristling of wet-rotten woods, mould-neglect, night-
    weather,
A hurt wildness stands there for help
And is saying something. Wild lumpy coat,
Greasy face-folds and sly eyes and a bandit abruptness,
Speech nearly not speech
Ducking under speech, asking for money
As if not asking. Huge storm-sky strangeness

And desperation. He knows he stands
In a shatter of your expectations. He waits for you
To feel through to his being alive.
He wants to flee. His cornered wildness
Dodges about in his eyes
That try to hide inside themselves, and his head jerks up
Trying to fit back together odd bits of dignity,
And he goes on, muttering, nodding, signalling OK OK.

Till you register: Money.

You give him bread, plastered with butter and piled with
    marmalade,
And stand watching him cram it into his mouth –
His wet, red, agile mouth
In the swollen collapsed face.
His grimed forefinger cocked.
A black column of frayed coat, belted with string,
Has surfaced for help.
Stares into the house-depth past you
Stranger than a snow-covered starving stag.

Munches, wipes his fingers on his coat, and wipes his
mouth
With the black-creased red palm.
A smile works his rubbery face
Like a hand working into a big glove.
His eyes wobble at you
Then an assault of launched eloquence
Like a sudden flooding of gratitude –
But you can't decode it.
He is extricating from his ponderous coat a topless bean-
can.
Spot o' tea in this ere, surr, if it's possible –

A prayer to be invisible,
Eyes flickering towards the road as if casually
He dips his lips to the scalding can's metal and sucks
Coolingly, hurriedly,
And now it comes again (the tossed-empty can back in his
pocket)
In a slither of thanks and salutes and shoulder-squarings
And sparring, feinting, dagger-stab glances
From the dissolved blue eyes
And the cornered mouse panic trying to slip into the house
past you –

MONEY!

Anaesthetic for the big body,
Its glistening full veins, its pumping organs,
Its great nerves to the eyes,
Unmanageable parcel of baggy pain
With its dry-sore brains, its tied rawness –

You give him your pocketful and he buries it without a
glance
And he's gone
Under his shoulder hunch, with hiding hands
And feet pretending no hurry
Under spattering and sneezing trees, over shining cobbles

To fall within two hundred yards
Dead-drunk in the church, to lie
Blowing, as if in post-operational shock,
Abandoned to space,
A lolling polyp of sweaty life, wrapped in its Guy Fawkes
    rags,
Bristling face-patch awry.

Ted Hughes

To the foot from its child

The child's foot is not yet aware it's a foot,
and would like to be a butterfly or an apple.

But in time, stones and bits of glass,
streets, ladders,
and the paths in the rough earth
go on teaching the foot that it cannot fly,
cannot be a fruit bulging on the branch.
Then, the child's foot
is defeated, falls
in the battle,
is a prisoner
condemned to live in a shoe.

Bit by bit, in that dark,
it grows to know the world in its own way,
out of touch with its fellow, enclosed,
feeling out life like a blind man.

These soft nails
of quartz, bunched together,
grow hard, and change themselves
into opaque substance, hard as horn,
and the tiny, petalled toes of the child
grow bunched and out of trim,
take on the form of eyeless reptiles
with triangular heads, like worms.
Later, they grow calloused
and are covered
with the faint volcanoes of death,
a coarsening hard to accept.

But this blind thing walks
without respite, never stopping
for hour after hour,
the one foot, the other,
now the man's,

now the woman's,
up above,
down below,
through fields, mines,
markets and ministries,
backwards,
far afield, inward,
forward,
this foot toils in its shoe,
scarcely taking time
to bare itself in love or sleep;
it walks, they walk,
until the whole man chooses to stop.

And then it descended
underground, unaware,
for there, everything, everything was dark.
It never knew it had ceased to be a foot
or if they were burying it so that it could fly
or so that it could become
an apple.

Pablo Neruda

Because the whole world was on fire

A little owlion named Tom Birkis Jonnes
And a shy gorillapple named Miss Hazel Hurryweather
Raced like mad all the way to the moviehouse
But it was some corny picture about these
Crooks riding on a train and an
Old woman keeps getting drunk so the
Ski troopers search everybody and just
At the border who should appear but
Twelve guys with hair on the outside
Of their hats and they don't even
Have a chance to start dealing when
A big dog in a jellyglass face suddenly
Comes on deck and machineguns the audience;
So Tom Birkis Jonnes and Miss Hazel Hurryweather
Were certainly glad they'd gone to the woods instead –
For there they met many nice friends and
Had much good talk and after a while
Got married and ate supper and some delicious pies.

Kenneth Patchen

Infant song

Don't you love my baby, mam,
Lying in his little pram,

Polished all with water clean,
The finest baby ever seen?

Daughter, daughter, if I could
I'd love your baby as I should,

But why the suit of signal red,
The horns that grow out of his head,

Why does he burn with brimstone heat,
Have cloven hooves instead of feet,

Fishing hooks upon each hand,
The keenest tail that's in the land,

Pointed ears and teeth so stark
And eyes that flicker in the dark?

Don't you love my baby, mam?

Dearest, I do not think I can.
I do not, do not think I can.

Charles Causley

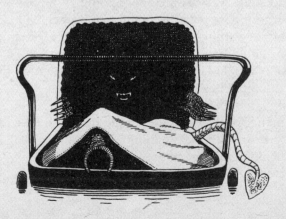

Any prince to any princess

August is coming
and the goose, I'm afraid,
is getting fat.
There have been
no golden eggs for some months now.
Straw has fallen well below market price
despite my frantic spinning
and the sedge is,
as you rightly point out,
withered.

I can't imagine how the pea
got under your mattress. I apologize
humbly. The chambermaid has, of course,
been sacked. As has the frog footman.
I understand that, during my recent fact-finding tour of the
    Golden River,
despite your nightly unavailing efforts,
he remained obstinately
froggish.

I hope that the Three Wishes granted by the General
    Assembly
will go some way towards redressing
this unfortunate recent sequence of events.
The fall in output from the shoe-factory, for example:
no one could have foreseen the work-to-rule
by the National Union of Elves. Not to mention the fact
that the court has been fast asleep
for the last six and a half years.
The matter of the poisoned apple has been taken up
by the Board of Trade: I think I can assure you
the incident will not be
repeated.

I can quite understand, in the circumstances,
your reluctance to let down
your golden tresses. However
I feel I must point out
that the weather isn't getting any better
and I already have a nasty chill
from waiting at the base
of the White Tower. You must see the absurdity of the
    situation.
Some of the courtiers are beginning to talk,
not to mention the humble villagers.
It's been three weeks now, and not even
a word.

Princess,
a cold, black wind
howls through our empty palace.
Dead leaves litter the bedchamber;
the mirror on the wall hasn't said a thing
since you left. I can only ask,
bearing all this in mind,
that you think again,

let down your hair,

reconsider.

Adrian Henri

From an Ecclesiastical Chronicle

In the year of Our Lord two thousand one hundred and
    seven,
The first electronic computer
Was appointed to a bishopric in the Church of England.
The consecration took place
At a Pontifical High Mass
In the new Cathedral of Stevenage,
In the presence of the Most Reverend
Mother in God, Her Grace Rita,
By Divine Connivance *Cantuar. Archepiscopissa.*

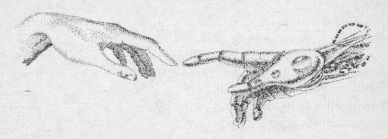

'Monsignor Pff-pff (75321/666)'
With notable efficiency, tact, and benevolence, presided
For the next three hundred years
Over his diocese. (He had previously worked
In the mission field – rural Dean of Callisto,
One of the satellites of Jupiter.)
After which he was honourably retired,
Only a little rusted, to the Science Museum
In South Kensington – there frequented and loved
By generations of schoolchildren.

At the *Times* remarked on that occasion
'He stood for the best in the Anglican tradition.'
In indubitable succession, one might say,
From our contemporary Dr –, of —.

John Heath-Stubbs

Index of first lines

Acknowledgements

John Betjeman
A Shropshire Lad
On a Portrait of a Deaf Man
Reprinted by permission of John Murray Ltd. (Publishers) from
John Betjeman *Collected Poems*

Elizabeth Bishop
The Man-Moth
The Fish
Reprinted by permission of Farrar, Straus & Giroux from *The Complete
Poems* by Elizabeth Bishop. Copyright © 1969 by Elizabeth Bishop

Ray Bradbury
Lo, The Ghost of Our Least Favourite Uncle
Reprinted by permission of the Harold Matson Co. (Agents) from *Where
Robot Mice and Robot Men Run Round in Robot Towns* by Ray Bradbury.
Copyright © 1979 by Ray Bradbury

Charles Causley
Timothy Winters
Infant Song
Ballad of the Breadman
The Forest of Tangle
Reprinted by permission of David Higham Associates (Agents) from
Collected Poems by Charles Causley

Alasdair Clayre
The Invisible Backwards Facing Grocer who Rose to Fame
Reprinted by permission of the author

Gregory Corso
The Last Gangster
Doll Poem
reprinted by permission of City Lights Books (Publishers) from *Gasoline*
by Gregory Corso. Copyright © 1958 by Gregory Corso

George MacBeth
The Day the World Ended
Bedtime Story
Reprinted by permission of the author

Roger McGough
Funny Sort of Bloke
Vague Impressions
Reprinted by permission of the author from *Holiday on Death Row* by
Roger McGough published by Jonathan Cape Ltd.
Pantomime Poem
Reprinted by permission of the author from *After the Merrymaking* by
Roger McGough published by Jonathan Cape Ltd.
George and the Dragonfly
Reprinted by permission of the author from *Gig* by Roger McGough
published by Jonathan Cape Ltd.

Spike Milligan
Scorflufus
Reprinted from *A Dustbin of Milligan* published by Star Books (W H
Allen and Co.)

Adrian Mitchell
The Castaways or Vote for Caliban
The Apeman who Hated Snakes
Reprinted by permission of Jonathan Cape Ltd. (Publishers) from
The Apeman Cometh by Adrian Mitchell
I Tried, I Really Tried
Nothingmas Day
Reprinted by permission of Cape Goliard Press (Publishers) from
Out Loud by Adrian Mitchell

Edwin Morgan
Spacepoem 3
Reprinted by permission of Edinburgh University Press (Publishers)
from *The Second Life* by Edwin Morgan

Christian Morgenstern
The Sparrow and the Kangaroo
In the Land of Punctuation
The Knee
Reprinted from *Christian Morgenstern's Galgenlieder, A Selection* translated by Max Knight, published by University of California Press, 1963

Susan Musgrave
Thrum Drew a Small Map
Reprinted from *Gullband* published by J J Douglas, Canada 1974

Pablo Neruda
To the Foot from its Child
Reprinted by permission of the Estate of Pablo Neruda from *Extravagaria* translated by Alistar Reed published by Jonathan Cape Ltd.

Kenneth Patchen
The Reason for Skylarks
Collected Poems of Kenneth Patchen. Copyright 1942 by New Directions Publishing Corporation. Reprinted by permission of New Directions, New York
Because the Whole World Was on Fire
Kenneth Patchen *Because It Is*. Copyright © 1960 by New Directions Publishing Corporation. Reprinted by permission of New Directions New York

Brian Patten
A Small Dragon
Reprinted from *Notes to the Hurrying Man* published by Allen and Unwin 1969
You'd Better Believe Him
Little Johnny's Confession
Reprinted from *Little Johnny's Confession* published by Allen and Unwin 1967
The Earth-ling
Reprinted by permission of the author

Mervyn Peake
from *Aunts and Uncles*
Reprinted by permission of Peter Owen Ltd. (Publishers) from *A Book of Nonsense* by Mervyn Peake

Kit Wright
The Fate of the Supermarket Manager
Reprinted by permission of Fontana Lions (Publishers) from *Rabbiting On*
by Kit Wright
A Doll's House
Reprinted by permission of the author from *The Bear Looked Over the Mountain* (Salamander Imprint) by Kit Wright

Ramsey Campbell
The Gruesome Book £1

Heartstopping, spinechilling tales to take your breath away. Begin your journey into nightmare with the horror of 'The Calling Card' and end it in the shocking terror of 'The Graveyard Rats'! A chillingly brilliant collection of truly gruesome stories. Warning: these stories are not to be read by the very young.

Amabel Williams-Ellis
The Story Spirits £1
folk tales from the Far East, Africa and the Caribbean

Once, long ago in one of the forests of Burma . . . Or was it Kampuchea? It could also have been Kenya, Ethiopia or Jamaica. This book will take you on a world trip filled with marvellous tales of evil spirits, kings and princesses, lions and tigers. Magical mystery tales of enchanted lands from China to Africa.

Michael de Larrabeiti
The Borribles £1.50

Borribles can be described as skinny, scruffy and quick-witted, with bright eyes, pointed ears and the bottoms hanging out of their trousers! But apart from that they look like normal children. While on look-out duty in Battersea Park, Knocker and Finger discover a Rumble. A Rumble on Borrible territory! The Borribles will need all their skill, stamina and initiative as the Great Rumble Hunt begins!

You can buy these and other Piccolo books from booksellers and newsagents; or direct from the following address:
Pan Books, Sales Office, Cavaye Place, London SW10 9PG
Send purchase price plus 35p for the first book and 15p for each additional book, to allow for postage and packing
Prices quoted are applicable in the UK

While every effort is made to keep prices low, it is sometimes necessary to increase prices at short notice. Pan Books reserve the right to show on covers and charge new retail prices which may differ from those advertised in the text or elsewhere